The Water Book

SECOND EDITION

Knapp

Water flowing to a new sewage
works on the River Ruhr

 ## Look after our environment!

It is easy to talk about looking after the environment, but we each have to help. Help often means small things, like not throwing waste into rivers. It doesn't take a lot of effort – just attitude.

Spray irrigation

A CVP Book
This second edition © Earthscape 2008

First edition 2002

Author
Brian Knapp, BSc, PhD

Art Director
Duncan McCrae, BSc

Senior Designer
Adele Humphries, BA, PGCE

Editors
*Lisa Magloff, MA,
and Gillian Gatehouse*

Designed and produced by
EARTHSCAPE

Printed in China by
WKT Company Ltd

**The Water Book Second Edition – Curriculum Visions
A CIP record for this book is
available from the British Library**

Paperback ISBN 978 1 86214 553 5

Illustrations
David Woodroffe

Picture credits
All photographs are from the Earthscape Picture Library, except the following (c=centre t=top b=bottom l=left r=right): *ShutterStock* cover, 17tl; *NOAA* 4–5.

Acknowledgements
The publishers would like to thank the following for their kind help and advice: *Thames Water plc (Farmoor Advanced Water Treatment Works and Oxford Sewage Treatment Works); Frank Sperling; the people of the Kiberagwe Community, Nairobi.*

This product is manufactured from sustainable managed forests. For every tree cut down at least one more is planted.

Contents

Glossary words
There is a glossary on page 47. Glossary terms
are referred to in the text by using **CAPITALS**.

Woman carrying drinking water, India

Introduction

Water is our most basic need, yet many people do not have enough. Cleaning up our water is a time consuming and expensive business.

1 There are many sources of water around us, some easy to spot, some very difficult. Find out what they are in the home on pages 6 and 7.

2 The water we use is continually moving from the oceans to the air to land and back to the oceans. This is called the **WATER CYCLE**. Find out how it works on pages 8 and 9.

3 Water reaches and leaves our homes in three ways. See what these are on pages 10 and 11.

4 The water in our taps is under pressure. See how this happens on pages 12 and 13.

5 Water is used far more for some purposes than others. Find out about the world's biggest water users on pages 14 and 15.

6 We control water by building **RESERVOIRS**. Reservoirs take up space and often force people from their homes. Some examples are given on pages 16 and 17.

7 Water is bulky and heavy to carry. This is why most of it is moved by rivers, canals and pipes, as you will find on pages 18 and 19.

8 In poorer countries many people have to go and fetch water for themselves. Find out what difficulties this causes on pages 20 and 21.

9 Much of the water we need is underground. This is clean water, but we can easily use it up as you will find on pages 22 and 23.

10 In some parts of the world water is not as plentiful as it is here. See what it is like in other places from where you live on pages 24 and 25.

⑪ Wildlife has to make the best of the water it can find. The ways wildlife adapts to a desert is shown on pages 26 and 27.

⑫ People who live in a desert have to adapt too. How they do this is shown on pages 28 and 29.

⑬ One of the worst things some people can suffer is a **DROUGHT**. See the ways poor people cope with this problem on pages 30 and 31.

⑭ We can all save some water. This means using less energy, saving land needed for reservoirs and saving money, as you can see on pages 32 and 33.

⑮ It is easy to make water dirty without even realising it. But once dirty it is difficult and expensive to clean. Find out about dirty water on pages 34 and 35.

⑯ Even today we cannot always take clean water for granted, yet it was often worse in the past. Find out how they managed on pages 36 and 37.

⑰ Cities were the first places to suffer from disease as a result of polluted water. Some horrific examples are given on pages 38 and 39.

⑱ Even today it is difficult to make water clean enough to drink. You can find out how it is done on pages 40 and 41.

⑲ We need to clean up any water we have **POLLUTED**. How this is done is shown on pages 42 and 43.

⑳ In poor countries there is very often too little money to clean up water the way we do. Some cheaper ways are shown on pages 44 and 45.

▼ A lesson from the past. In the 1930s farmers in the west of the United States did not understand how best to use the water that came naturally. So when a drought came, the crops died and the soil blew away. They called this land the Dust Bowl. You can see why in this picture taken at the time.

Water around us

We can find water doing many jobs around us, both inside and outside.

Where can you find water? To answer this question, let's start indoors and then look outside.

Water indoors

We can easily find water if we turn on a tap. Water comes into the kitchen where it fills sinks (picture ①), washing machines and dishwashers. It comes in through the shower and taps in the bath (picture ②) and, through an outside tap, supplies the hose in the garden (picture ③).

Water also comes into the toilet. It stays in the toilet bowl and in the cistern behind it, and flows out into pipes called **SEWERS** when we pull the flush.

There is water in our tea, in other drinks, in our food and we use water when we do most of our cooking.

Out of sight (and often in the loft) there will also be a large tank that stores water for the whole house. All of these are sources of **DRINKING WATER**.

◀▼ ① **Water is used in many ways around a kitchen.**

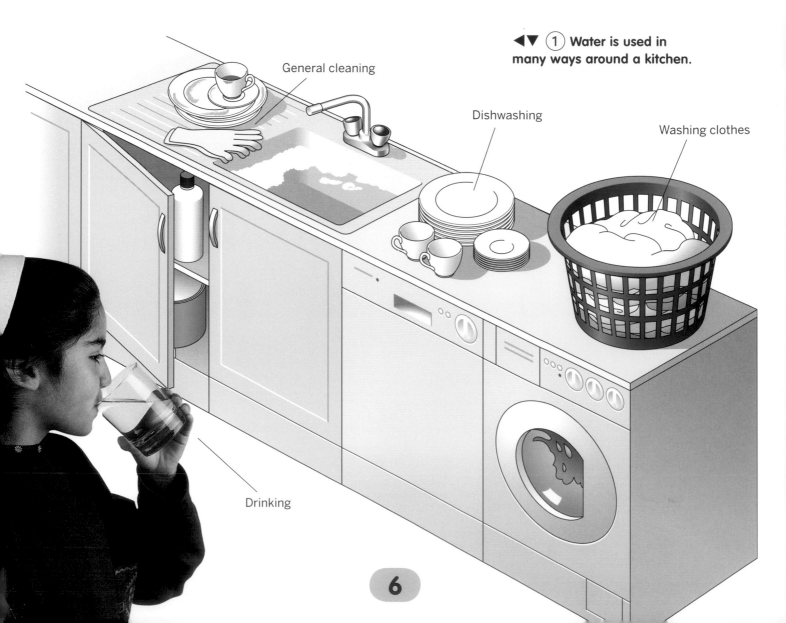

General cleaning

Dishwashing

Washing clothes

Drinking

▼ ② Places where you find water in a bathroom.

At school there may also be a swimming pool.

Water outside

If it rains, then roofs, roads and school playgrounds get wet. Water flows to gutters before disappearing in underground drains.

Coming in, going out

As you look at all of these sources of water, you may have noticed that water is not used up. For example, water is used for washing, for a shower, a bath or the toilet, but although we may make water dirty, we never use it up. So where does the water come from and what happens when we have used it and made it dirty?

▼ ③ Places where you find water in a garden.

Weblink: www.CurriculumVisions.com

Where water comes from

The water we use at home has to come from nature – from rivers and from underground.

All of the water in our taps comes from nature – the environment around us. To know where to look for water, it is important to understand how water moves around the Earth.

The water cycle

Water is continually moving about (e.g. flowing in rivers) and changing from one form to another (e.g. evaporating from oceans). We call this never-ending movement of natural water around the world the **WATER CYCLE** (picture ①).

Making use of the water cycle

By understanding the water cycle we can see that we can use water from the ground as well as from rivers and lakes. We will see how this is done in the next part of the book.

▼▶ ① The natural water cycle. Notice that water changes from a liquid to a gas (vapour) and back to a liquid. It is never used up.

2. Clouds

There is water vapour in the air around you now, but it is so thinly spread that you cannot see it. However, high in the cold clouds, moisture forms into tiny droplets which then grow large enough to fall from the air as rain (or snow if the air is very cold).

1. The oceans

Well over nine-tenths of the world's water is in the oceans. However, we can't drink this water because it contains lots of salt. Liquid water changes to invisible water vapour due to the warmth of the air and the heat from the Sun. This is known as EVAPORATION.

The water vapour that rises from the oceans has no salt in it. This will form the fresh water that we can drink.

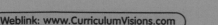

3. Rain

Rainwater is pure water – it is not salty and is normally quite safe to drink. But it is not easy to catch. When rain falls, most of it immediately sinks into the soil. However, some other living things are better able to use it than us. Most important are plants, which suck up water from the soil through their roots.

4. Rocks

Any rain not used by plants seeps into the ground, first through tho coil and then into the rocks below. Water moves very slowly through the rocks. It may take weeks or months to travel to a river.

5. Rivers and lakes

Once the rocks are full, water begins to seep out at the surface, perhaps as SPRINGS, but mostly unseen through the beds of rivers and lakes. This (not rainfall) is the main source of water for most rivers.

Finally, rivers carry the water back to sea and so complete the water cycle.

6. Floods

Only during the heaviest rain, or after the wettest of seasons, do we ever see water flowing on the surface. When it does this we call the surface water a FLOOD.

Water coming and going

We use water for many things. But we never use it up so we have to keep getting rid of the dirty water.

We use clean water to drink. But we also make water dirty. Rain adds a kind of water that is not completely clean or dirty.

To keep all of these kinds of water separate we need three sets of pipes:
- the pipes that give us clean water;
- the pipes that carry away waste water; and
- the pipes that carry away rainwater.

Clean water

Clean water is provided by a **WATER COMPANY** (picture ①).

The water company pumps water under pressure – first through main supply pipes. These pipes branch and branch again into smaller pipes so that eventually everyone gets their own supply.

Waste water

Once we have used water, it is unsafe to drink. It is important that it goes in completely separate pipes from the clean water (pictures ② and ③). These are called **SEWERS**.

Because waste water contains solid pieces such as scraps from the kitchen and toilet waste, waste pipes leaving our homes need to be ten times the size of clean water pipes.

▼ ① **How clean water gets to our homes.**

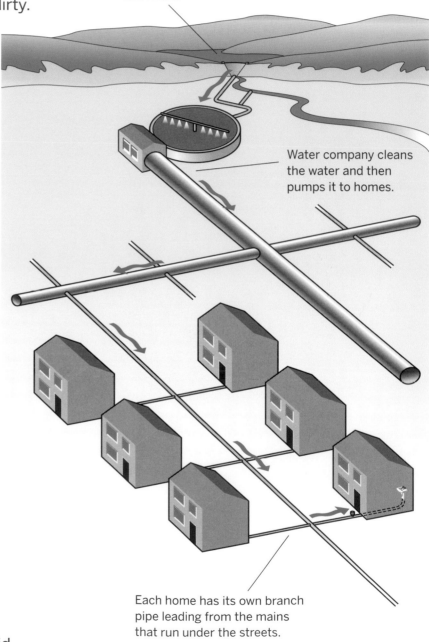

Water from reservoirs and rivers.

Water company cleans the water and then pumps it to homes.

Each home has its own branch pipe leading from the mains that run under the streets.

The pipes that reach our taps are just 15mm across, but because the water is under pressure, when you turn the tap on water gushes out.

15mm

Waste water goes to the **SEWAGE TREATMENT WORKS** where it is made clean again (for more on this see pages 42 and 43).

▶ ③ **Water pipes run under our streets. The largest are sewers, the next largest are drinking water mains.**

▼ ② **How waste water leaves our homes.**

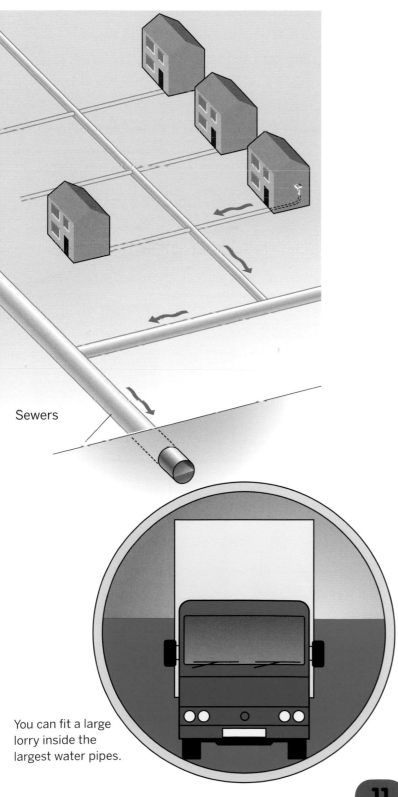

Sewers

You can fit a large lorry inside the largest water pipes.

Rainwater

Rainfall is sometimes so heavy that we need separate pipes to drain rainwater (picture ④). If we used the sewer pipes, they could fill up after heavy rain and flood out into the streets.

▼ ④ **How rainwater is carried way.**

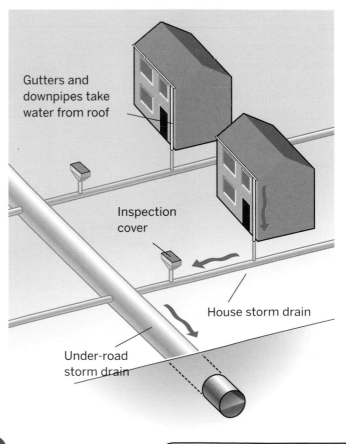

Gutters and downpipes take water from roof

Inspection cover

House storm drain

Under-road storm drain

Weblink: www.CurriculumVisions.com

Building up pressure

Not every place gets pumped water. In many places people get their water from large tanks that store water above ground level.

If you want to get water to move quickly, it must be under pressure. This can be done by pumping water using high-pressure pumps. It can also be done using tanks (picture ①).

How you get your water

In your home there may be a big cold-water storage tank. If you live in a house it will be in the loft. If you live in a flat it will be in the roof above the uppermost floor.

Water comes in from the mains under pressure. It is pumped from the water company and fed to the tank. The tank does two jobs: it holds a reserve of water if the

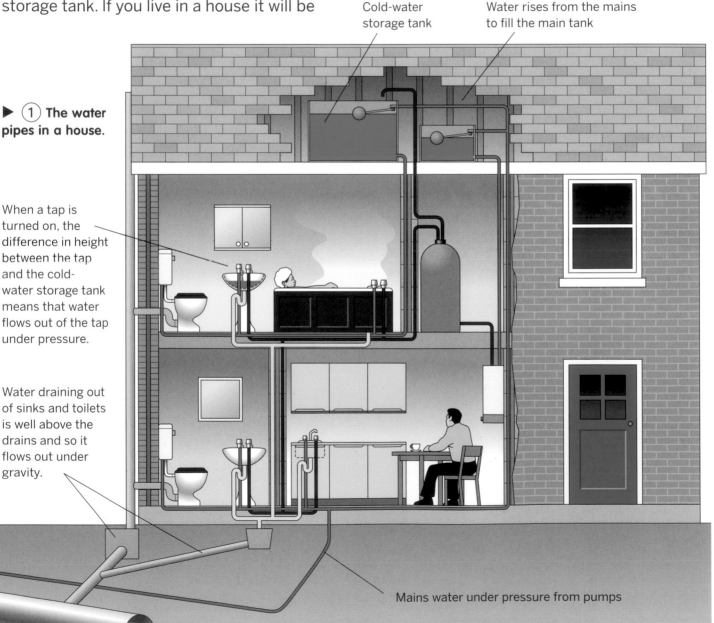

▶ ① **The water pipes in a house.**

Cold-water storage tank

Water rises from the mains to fill the main tank

When a tap is turned on, the difference in height between the tap and the cold-water storage tank means that water flows out of the tap under pressure.

Water draining out of sinks and toilets is well above the drains and so it flows out under gravity.

Mains water under pressure from pumps

mains pumps fail, and it also cuts down the pressure, meaning that joints in pipes are less likely to spring leaks. However, the tank still needs to be high enough above the taps in order to give enough pressure for the water to flow quickly. This is why it is in the loft.

When you turn on a tap, the water flows from the tank, through all of the pipes, and out of the tap.

Community tanks

In some places water is not pumped directly to homes. Instead, tanks are used to provide water pressure to the people nearby (pictures ② and ③).

▼▶ ② and ③. **A water tower is designed to make sure that the tank is well above any roof top. This means that the water will flow from the tower to the nearby houses quickly. Community tanks are often fed by water pumped from the ground. The tanks are covered to make sure germs are kept out.**

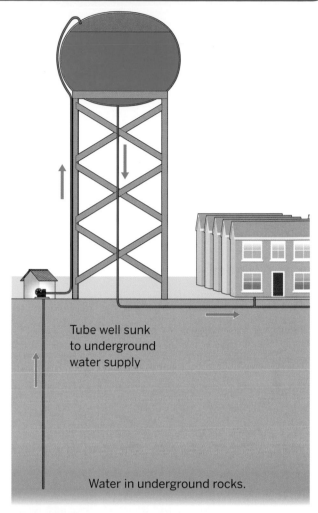

Tube well sunk to underground water supply

Water in underground rocks.

Big users!

We don't use the most water in our homes. In many countries farmers and power companies use far more.

Although there are billions of us, we still do not use as much water at home as power stations and farmers. For these other users, water does not have to be clean enough to drink. This is just as well, because the world's biggest users gulp it down in gigantic quantities.

Water for power

Power stations that make electricity from flowing water are called **HYDROELECTRIC POWER STATIONS** (picture ①). They can 'swallow' whole rivers. Coal, oil and gas power stations

▼ ① **Hydroelectric power stations use so much water that a dam and reservoir often have to be built just to supply their needs. This dam is on the Colorado River in the USA.**

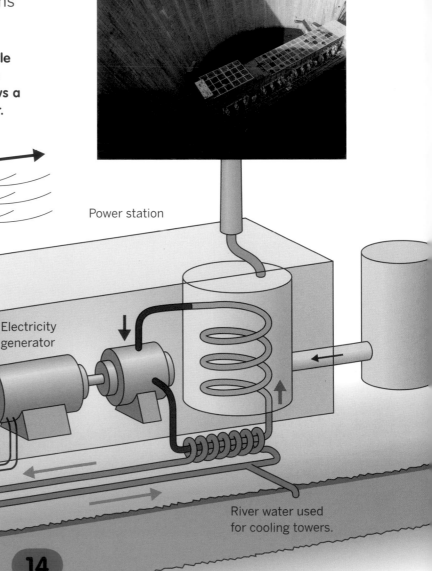

Reservoir

Dam

▼ ② **Cooling towers try to recycle water, but even so they use large amounts. This picture below shows a power station beside a large river.**

Cooling tower

Power station

Electricity generator

River water used for cooling towers.

▼ ③ Farmers can easily waste water if they simply use it to flood fields. This is known as flood irrigation.

need water to keep their generators cool. This is why they use cooling towers (picture ②). Some power stations are placed close to rivers so they can also use river water to cool their generators.

Water for food

Farmers in hot, dry areas such as China, Egypt, Russia, Pakistan, India, Australia and parts of the United States have an enormous demand for water. They are the world's biggest users of water (pictures ③ and ④) and they use it for **IRRIGATION**. Far more **RESERVOIRS** are built to store water for these farmers than for any other purpose.

Unlike power stations, which can be built near rivers, farmers have to work fertile soil wherever it occurs.

▼ ④ Less water is used if water is sprayed on, or even drip fed to the plant roots. Spraying is more expensive than flooding, so it is not common in poorer countries.

Often this is far from rivers. River water therefore has to be diverted to farmland – usually by canal. But in some places water can be found in underground rocks (see page 22).

Reservoirs

To make sure we have enough water in times of drought, we need to store some of the surplus from times when there is plentiful rain. We can do this using reservoirs.

A reservoir is an artificial lake with a dam at one end (pictures ①, ② and ③).

Reservoirs are important if people are to have enough water. In a country like the UK, where rain falls in every month, reservoirs are built to prevent shortages during the few weeks each year when rain is a bit less than would normally be expected.

Some countries, however, have very long, dry periods (see pages 24 to 25). In countries such as these, the need for water is much greater and so the reservoirs are much larger.

Valley is flooded to make reservoir.

These beach lines show how the water has been let out of the reservoir.

The reservoir is full by the end of the winter.

Steep banks with no floodplain.

The reservoir is at a low level by the end of the summer.

The flow of water is adjusted by opening sluice gates in the dam.

The dam is built where the valley is narrow to make it easier and cheaper to construct. A deeper valley means that more water can be stored in a smaller area, and less land is affected, so dams are mostly found in mountainous areas.

▲ ① **Reservoirs are managed. They are allowed to become fairly empty just before winter, and they are filled just before summer. You can tell whether the reservoir is empty or full by looking for the 'beach' lines. If you see no beach lines, the reservoir is full.**

▼ ② This is the Craig Goch reservoir in Wales. It is a moderately-sized reservoir with a moderately-sized dam blocking a steep-sided, deep valley – a typical site.

Water takes up a lot of space, however, and so even storing a small amount uses up lots of land. All of the reservoirs in the UK, for example, hold just two-hundredths of the amount of water used in a year. There is no need to store more water because of the high cost and the loss of land that would be flooded.

Where to build a reservoir

A reservoir must be built in a place where there is reliable water – in the mountains, for example, or across the path of a large river. But not every place will do. For example, a reservoir must not lie over rocks that soak up water!

There are few reservoirs near to cities because people will want to use the land for other things.

▲ ③ The Roosevelt Dam, Salt River, Arizona, USA. Compare it to the drawing opposite.

Very large reservoirs

We could store more water, but the more we store, the more land would be flooded and the less land there would be for farming. Even some villages and towns might be flooded if we used more land for reservoirs.

17

How we move water

Places of plentiful water are often far from places where people live. As a result, water has to be moved long distances.

We use huge amounts of water. Some of it we get directly from rivers, the rest is moved in canals (picture ①) or underground pipes (picture ②).

There are water pipes under every city street. You only notice how much water is flowing in these hidden pipes when a main pipe bursts and water pushes the soil and road surface up. A burst main carries more than enough clean water to flood a street.

Water is bulky and heavy

You soon realise this if you try to carry a full watering can about, perhaps from a garden tap to a flower bed.

People used to know the rhyme "a pint of water weighs a pound and a quarter". Translated into metric this means that a litre of water weighs a kilogram. A watering can holds about 5 litres, or 5kg of water.

◀ ① **Modern aqueducts are huge concrete-lined canals. This is the California aqueduct in the United States. It is 12m wide at the base, 10m deep and 440km long.**

▼ ② **Water pipes are large and expensive. The trees help you see the size of the pipe leading from this water tunnel.**

MOFFAT - WATER - TUNNEL

You might use over a hundred litres (20 watering cans full) of water a day (washing, cooking, flushing the toilet, etc.). Just imagine carrying 20 watering cans of water every day of your life! It takes up time and is hard work. This is why we use canals, tunnels and pipes to move the water we use.

Moving water by canal

If there is no river nearby, the best way of moving large amounts of water over long distances is to use an **AQUEDUCT**. This is a canal used only for carrying water.

Modern aqueducts are huge. California has the most extensive system of large modern canals in the world.

Moving drinking water by river

There is a cheaper way of moving water than by canal. If the places where water is stored (in reservoirs) are on the same river as where it is needed (in cities), then the river can be used as a kind of free aqueduct. The water can then be taken from the river near the city and cleaned for use (picture ③).

▼ ③ **The world's rivers carry 66 million cubic metres of water each second. This river is being used as a free aqueduct, carrying water from a reservoir in the mountains to the city.**

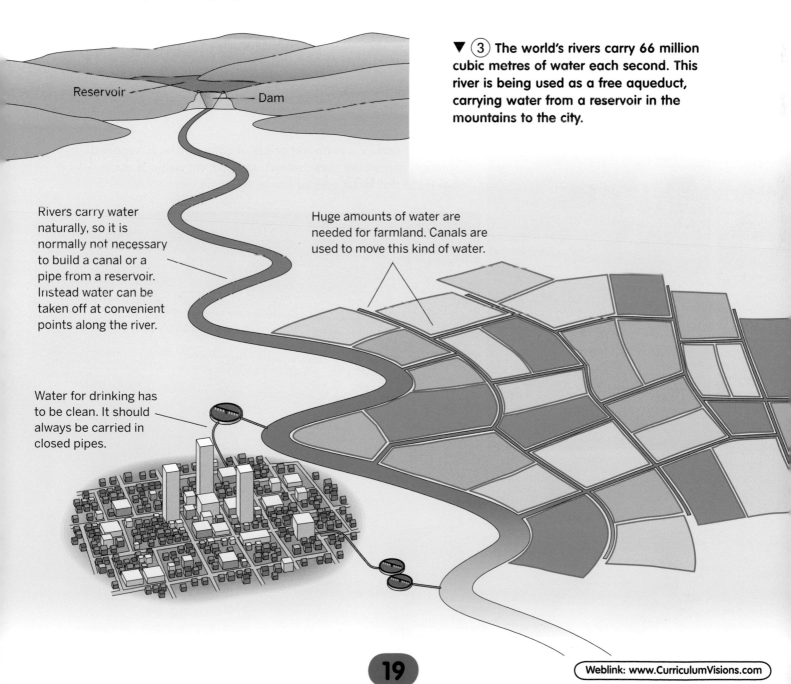

Reservoir — Dam

Rivers carry water naturally, so it is normally not necessary to build a canal or a pipe from a reservoir. Instead water can be taken off at convenient points along the river.

Huge amounts of water are needed for farmland. Canals are used to move this kind of water.

Water for drinking has to be clean. It should always be carried in closed pipes.

Moving water in poorer countries

Aqueducts and pipes are too expensive for many poor countries. Instead, people have to carry their own water – and the water they get may not even be clean.

People who live in prosperous countries can afford to clean water thoroughly and send it by pipes to every home. But poorer countries cannot afford all of this. As a result, many people do not get clean water piped to them, or waste water taken away.

Communal water

The biggest cost is in providing pipes and a tap to every home. So money can be saved by using communal taps. This means that people still get clean water, but they have to fetch and carry their water between the communal taps and their homes. This is quite common in poor areas of big cities in **DEVELOPING COUNTRIES** (pictures ① and ②).

◄▼ ① and ②. In poorer areas of cities, water is supplied through communal taps (below). At least the water is clean, but it still has to be carried home (left).

▼ ③ Collecting water from a river. This is not a clean source of water. Water-borne diseases are a serious worldwide problem. Almost 250 million people each year contract a water-borne disease, and about 10 million of them die from such diseases.

▼ ④ A boy collecting water from the bottom of a pit dug in the ground. This is a kind of shallow well.

▼ ⑤ If people are very poor they may not even be able to afford a plastic container. In this picture gourds are used as natural containers.

Very often it is the women in a family that do the backbreaking work of collecting water.

No water

If there is even less money, there can be no pipes at all. This is what it is like in many rural areas in poorer parts of the world.

Because there are no pipes, people now have to get water from wherever they can find it – water that may not be clean and which may be a long way away (pictures ③, ④, ⑤ and ⑥). People now find themselves carrying water for hours a day – time they could otherwise spend growing food or going to school.

▼ ⑥ When water has to be carried many kilometres, a donkey provides welcome help.

Using water in the ground

Many rocks naturally store huge amounts of water. This water can be pumped directly from the ground.

The rocks below our feet can be natural 'sponges'. Water in the ground is called **GROUNDWATER**.

Rocks get their water from rain. Once the rocks are full, the rest spills out and makes springs.

Springs occur all around the edges of water-storing rocks, or **AQUIFERS**.

Groundwater is clean water

Any rainwater stored underground stays free from mud and germs. This is one reason spring waters have always been highly prized.

Wells

You don't need to go to a spring to use underground water. Instead, you can dig a **WELL** (pictures ① and ②).

When the well is dug deep enough, water will seep from the rock into the well.

For centuries, people got their water this way. Hundreds of millions still do.

The advantages of groundwater

Storing the water underground takes up no space on the surface (unlike reservoirs), and the water is clean and reliable (pictures ③ and ④). This means that many people can get a water supply without having to be connected together by pipes. This is especially important to farmers and people living in the countryside. However, it still costs money to dig a well.

▼ ① and ②. Wells are the traditional way of taking water from the ground.

Well

Water-storing rock

Limits to using groundwater

There is a huge amount of water stored in rocks. Water-holding rocks are also not found everywhere. This is why we often cannot use the water stored in the ground as our only supply.

▶ ③ **This is a wind-powered water pump over a well. It is in a rural area and it is designed to pump water for cattle to drink.**

▼ ④ **If water-holding rocks are trapped between two watertight rock layers, the water filling up the aquifer comes under pressure. It is then called ARTESIAN WATER. This water can be released by drilling wells. This makes a water supply that, at least to begin with, does not require pumps to bring it to the surface.**

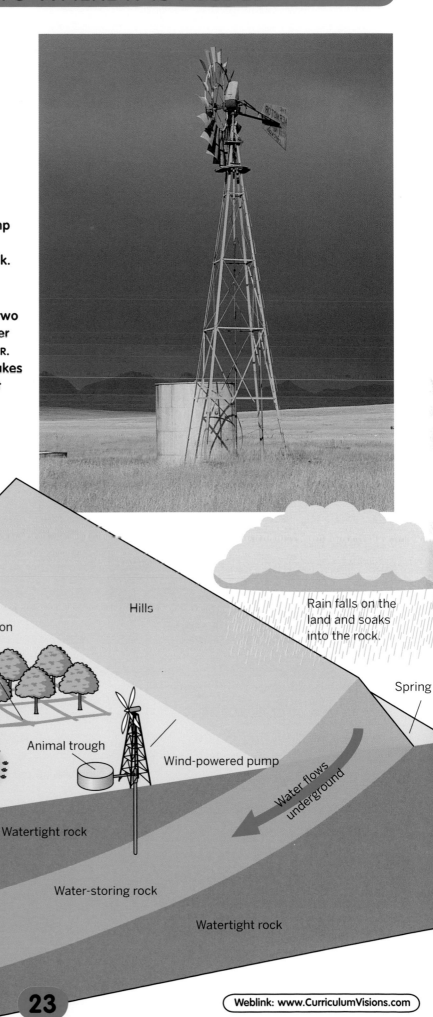

Rain falls on the land and soaks into the rock.

Hills

Spring

Flood irrigation

Spray irrigation

Animal trough

Wind-powered pump

Water flows underground

Watertight rock

Water-storing rock

Watertight rock

Groundwater

Water is drawn from the ground, disinfected if necessary and then piped to towns and cities.

Weblink: www.CurriculumVisions.com

Why worry about water?

Water may seem plentiful to us, but it is not the same everywhere in the world.

Worrying about water may seem really strange. After all, for most of us it often seems we have too much of it.

Just occasionally we understand how much we depend on water, when the rainfall is low and the rivers and reservoirs begin to dry up. We call this a drought. But, all in all, we live in a well-watered part of the world, whereas many other people do not (picture ①). It is they who will run short of water first.

Water is more important even than food. You would die from thirst long before you would die from hunger. In the future, finding, using and conserving water will become more important than finding new supplies of oil. On the following pages you will see how wildlife copes with too little water, and then how people survive in deserts and in places where rain is unreliable and droughts are common. Finally, you can find out how we can make better use of our water, too.

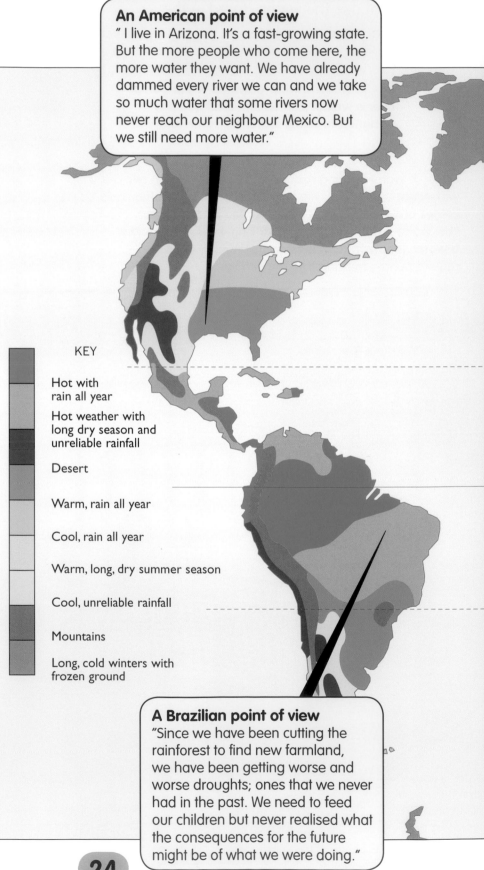

An American point of view
" I live in Arizona. It's a fast-growing state. But the more people who come here, the more water they want. We have already dammed every river we can and we take so much water that some rivers now never reach our neighbour Mexico. But we still need more water."

KEY

Hot with rain all year

Hot weather with long dry season and unreliable rainfall

Desert

Warm, rain all year

Cool, rain all year

Warm, long, dry summer season

Cool, unreliable rainfall

Mountains

Long, cold winters with frozen ground

A Brazilian point of view
"Since we have been cutting the rainforest to find new farmland, we have been getting worse and worse droughts; ones that we never had in the past. We need to feed our children but never realised what the consequences for the future might be of what we were doing."

PROVIDING WATER TO A THIRSTY WORLD

▼ ① The Earth contains about 1.4 billion cubic kilometres of water. But 97% of it is in the world's oceans – and all of this is salty and unusable! 2% is locked up in the world's ice sheets. Most of the rest is in the world's rocks. The water flowing in rivers is just one four-thousandth of the world's fresh water.

On average, people throughout the world use about 60 litres of water per day. The easier it is to obtain water, and the cheaper the water is to buy, the more we use. For those who have to carry their own water, like many people in places like Madagascar, home use can be as low as 6 litres a day. But when water is easy to obtain, use rises dramatically. In the UK we each use about 150 litres a day and in the United States, where water is very cheap, people use 380 litres per person per day for their home needs.

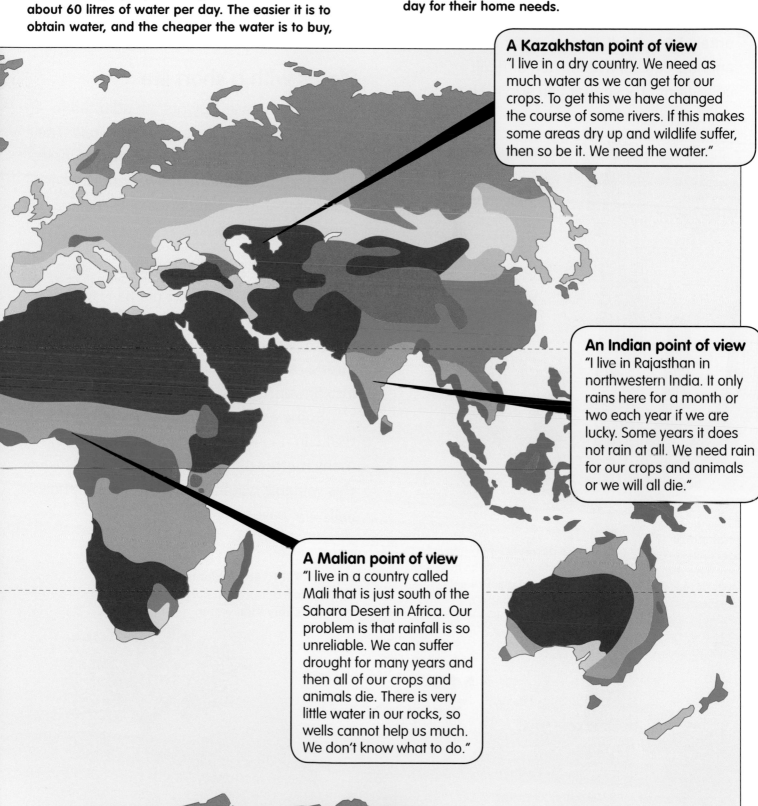

A Kazakhstan point of view
"I live in a dry country. We need as much water as we can get for our crops. To get this we have changed the course of some rivers. If this makes some areas dry up and wildlife suffer, then so be it. We need the water."

An Indian point of view
"I live in Rajasthan in northwestern India. It only rains here for a month or two each year if we are lucky. Some years it does not rain at all. We need rain for our crops and animals or we will all die."

A Malian point of view
"I live in a country called Mali that is just south of the Sahara Desert in Africa. Our problem is that rainfall is so unreliable. We can suffer drought for many years and then all of our crops and animals die. There is very little water in our rocks, so wells cannot help us much. We don't know what to do."

How wildlife survives in a desert

Deserts have the least water of anywhere in the world. To stay alive, plants and animals have to adapt.

Deserts are mainly hot places with very unreliable rainfall. Very few plants and animals can survive in such difficult conditions. Those that can survive have to be specially adapted to hold on to whatever moisture they can get (picture ①).

Plants with a short life

Two types of desert plants are adapted to desert life. One group is called annuals. Their seeds lie in the desert soil until rain comes. Then, they race to grow, flower and set seed – all before the ground dries out. This may all happen in a few weeks.

Plants that grow slowly

The other group of desert plants is called perennials. During the long periods without rain, they simply stop growing. Then, just after a rainstorm, they grow leaves and burst into flower.

Some desert perennials have deep roots that can find water even when it has seeped many metres underground. To prevent losing this valuable water, such plants have small, leathery leaves.

Some birds can get water (as well as food) from the stem of the cactus.

The cactus is a valuable store of water for animals. To protect itself against animals this cactus has hard spines.

The saguaro cactus stores water in its stem. It has no leaves as these increase the amount of water lost to the hot, dry desert air.

A desert fox can survive by getting most of its moisture from the plants it eats.

▼ ① **Some plants and animals are adapted to survive where there is very little water.**

The cactus has a network of roots close to the surface to catch any rain that might seep into the soil from a passing storm.

Plants such as this creosote bush have very deep roots to find water. As with many plants in the desert, they also have small, leathery leaves.

Other plants, such as the cactus, store water in fleshy stems. They have no leaves at all; their green stems make all the food they need (picture ②).

◄ ② Cacti store water in their fleshy stems.

Animals that use no water

Some animals can survive on hardly any water (picture ③). The kangaroo rat is one of these. It can get all of the moisture it needs from the food it eats. However, it makes sure it stays out of the hot daytime sun and, like most desert animals, it is only active at night.

▼ ③ A desert beetle climbs to the top of a sand dune in the Namib Desert to catch the precious early morning mist.

Animals that store water

Camels can eat the toughest and thorniest plants, they can eat the leaves and twigs of shrubs, and grasses that would look dead to us (picture ④). The food is stored in the hump on their backs and can be turned into water in times of need. Camels can drink up to 100 litres of water. By these two means they can survive without water for more than two weeks. Unlike people, camels are able to lose up to a quarter of their body weight without becoming ill.

◄ ④ Camels have some of the most extraordinary ways of storing water.

Weblink: www.CurriculumVisions.com

How people live in a desert

People do not naturally have the adaptations of desert animals, so they must find other ways of getting water.

Because it is so hard to find water, few people live in a desert. The only places where large numbers of people live in a desert is where a river flows from a wetter region through a desert. The people who live by the River Nile in Egypt are a good example.

There is no point in planning for the use of rain in a desert. Any people who live in a desert must find much more reliable sources. Those who live away from rivers must look for water in rocks.

▼ ① **Oases, such as this one in Morocco, are the most reliable places to find water, but they cannot support many people.**

Oases

In a few places there are natural springs. These make water holes called **OASES** (picture ①).

Few oases have enough water for large numbers of people to grow crops, as well as provide for their own needs.

To get more water into the desert, some governments have drilled deep wells into the rocks below the desert. This has been done, for example, in the North African country of Libya. As a result, large areas of crops can be grown in land that was once barren desert.

Clothes

To survive with limited amounts of water means losing as little water from your skin as possible. This is one reason that desert people often wear loose-fitting clothing that covers them from head to toe (picture ②). The clothing stops air blowing across the skin and taking moisture away.

Emergency survival

In an emergency there are many ways to survive in a desert – if you know how. You could, for example, look for plants that store water in underground stems. You could also collect dew. Dew can be collected at night, when the desert air cools, by making a funnel shape from a plastic sheet. The dew forms by a process called **CONDENSATION**. Any dew that forms on the sheet will drain to the bottom of the funnel.

It is even possible to separate the water out of your urine (picture ③). You can do this using the heat from the Sun. It works by a process called **DISTILLATION**. The urine is placed in a container and allowed to heat up and evaporate in the heat of the Sun. This leaves all of the unwanted impurities in the bottom of the container. The evaporated (clean) water condenses on a plastic sheet placed over the container. Now it can be drunk again!

▶ ② **Many desert-living people cover their bodies to prevent excessive loss of moisture in the dry heat.**

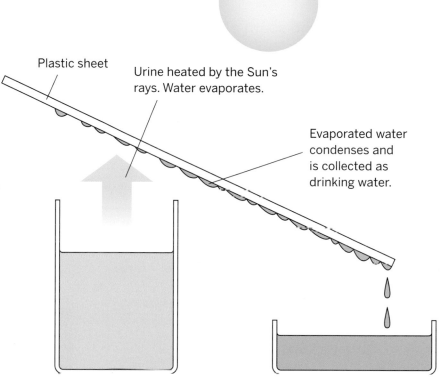

▼ ③ **Getting drinking water from urine for desert survival.**

Plastic sheet

Urine heated by the Sun's rays. Water evaporates.

Evaporated water condenses and is collected as drinking water.

Places with drought

Much of the world has very unreliable rainfall. The people who live in such places need to cope with this. Here is what happens in parts of Africa.

Much of the land south of Africa's Sahara Desert is not a desert, but it has unreliable rainfall. In some years there is enough rain for crops, in other years there is not. This is actually a far worse situation than living in a desert. In a desert you know you will get no rain – here you hope you will, but you may not.

Catching precious rainwater

Far more people live in this kind of land than in a desert. So if the rains fail, very large numbers are at risk.

This means that the people have to try to save as much rain as they can. Yet when the rain falls, it falls so heavily that it does not have time to soak into the soil, and the people are in danger of losing the water before it has had time to do any good.

▼ ① **By digging small ridges, or soil dams, across a slope, rainwater can be ponded to give it more time to seep into the soil.**

▼ ② **A village comes together to dig ditches designed to trap rainwater.**

Soil dams

One way to hold back rainwater is to dig ditches across the land and pile the soil from the ditch up to make a mini-dam (pictures ① and ②). This gives time for the water to soak in.

Dams, ponds and concrete jars

How do the people store enough water for themselves? One answer is to make small dams on local rivers and store water behind them (picture ③). Another way is to collect water from roofs and keep it in ponds beside their homes. The ponds need to be covered over to stop the water evaporating.

▼ ③ This small dam will not store enough water for crops, but it will help give people enough water to drink until the next rains come.

▼ ④ A concrete jar built to collect rainwater. Aid agencies help provide the money for such simple ways of storing water.

Yet another way is to use tall, concrete jars with a tap near the bottom (picture ④). Water from roof gutters can be used to fill these up during the rainy season. It is not a huge amount to our eyes, but when people are careful with their water, a jar like this can hold enough to last a family one or two months.

Weblink: www.CurriculumVisions.com

Saving water

In the future, saving water will become more and more important. Much of what can be done is easy and just needs a little thought.

In many parts of the world water is already in short supply. It also costs money to clean up dirty water. So is it possible to cut down on the amount we use and, if so, how can we do it?

How farms can save water

Farms need lots of water. The simplest way of providing it is to flood the fields. This is also the most wasteful way because a lot of the water evaporates and is lost to the air.

It saves huge amounts of water if farmers use a sprinkler and even more if they use pipes that run beside plant roots (picture ①).

How water companies can save water

Water companies look after an enormous network of pipes. As pipes get old, many break or leak at the joints. Leaks waste billions of litres of water a day (picture ②). By repairing leaks, water companies can play a major part in saving water.

Water companies take all of our **POLLUTED WATER** from our sewers, clean it and put it back into rivers for reuse. This is a vital way to save water.

◄ ① The sprinkler nozzles on this pipe will spray just the right amount of water down onto the roots. Spraying takes place at night when there is least evaporation.

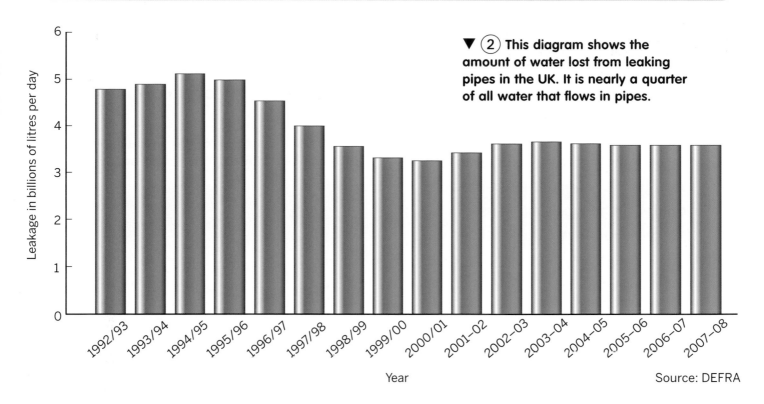

▼ ② **This diagram shows the amount of water lost from leaking pipes in the UK. It is nearly a quarter of all water that flows in pipes.**

Source: DEFRA

How we can save water

We can also help to save water. We can use toilets that flush with less water (picture ③) and we can use showers instead of baths. A shower (but not a power shower) uses a tenth of the water compared to a bath.

▼ ③ **Using less water for flushing saves money. One way to save water is to put a brick in the cistern.**

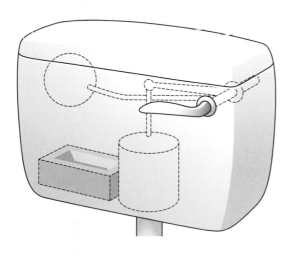

We can also use less water on our gardens and put it only on the flowers, not on the grass (picture ④).

These ways of saving mean that water companies have to spend less on cleaning water and less on new reservoirs. So the more we save, the less we get charged for our water and the less land we lose as reservoirs.

▼ ④ **A garden sprinkler uses about 15 litres of water a minute – about the same as a person in a poor country must carry to meet their daily needs.**

Where pollution comes from

There are many causes of pollution. Some are easier to control than others.

When people say that water is dirty, they don't just mean that it contains things that turn it brown. They also mean that it contains chemicals, such as oil and detergents, or **GERMS** that make it unhealthy. A better word for dirty water is **POLLUTED WATER** (picture ①).

Pollution

All water contains some chemicals. Therefore, no naturally occurring water is absolutely pure. In fact, some people prefer to drink bottled 'mineral' water because the chemicals in it give the water a pleasant taste.

Pollution is when unwanted and unhealthy substances get into the water. This is still a big problem in many rivers where the river is used as a cheap form of **SEWER** (picture ②) or dumping ground (picture ③).

▼ ② **A lot of pollution comes from dumping raw sewage into rivers, lakes or the sea.**

▼ ① **Some of the sources of pollution.**

This kind of pollution is hard to control

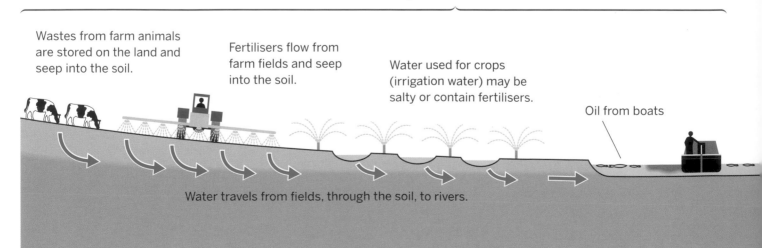

Wastes from farm animals are stored on the land and seep into the soil.

Fertilisers flow from farm fields and seep into the soil.

Water used for crops (irrigation water) may be salty or contain fertilisers.

Oil from boats

Water travels from fields, through the soil, to rivers.

Human and farm pollution

Human and animal wastes contain unhealthy germs.

Human wastes and farm fertilisers also provide lots of nourishment for microscopic water plants (algae), which is why they grow rapidly in polluted water. As they grow, they take oxygen from the water, making it impossible for the water to clean itself.

Factory wastes

In some countries rivers become polluted by factory wastes (picture ④). Some wastes contain harmful chemicals, others contain metals that are poisonous to river life and to people.

▶ ④ You can sometimes spot chemical pollution because the water is a strange colour or it has froth on the surface. However, pollution can be invisible, too.

▼ ③ Some people treat rivers, lakes and the sea as a rubbish dump.

This kind of pollution is easier to control

Wastes from factories are often highly polluted and need to be treated by special means. This is often done on the factory premises.

Waste from home toilets and sinks will cause pollution if it goes straight to rivers. It is usually collected in pipes and taken to sewage works. In country areas, without mains pipes, each house has its own underground septic tank. From time to time, the sewage is collected and taken to a sewage works.

Oil from cars

Rainwater is often allowed to go straight to rivers. It does, however, contain materials washed off streets and roofs. It would not be fit to drink, but it is a very small source of pollution.

Getting clean water: the early years

Water has to be clean to be healthy – and this is how people started cleaning water.

When we turn on a tap, we take it for granted that the water is clean and good for us. But it was not always like this, and in many parts of the world the water is still not safe to drink.

Living in the country

For many thousands of years people lived in small groups spread out around the countryside. During this time they did nothing special to clean their water, but in general the water was clean and safe to use (picture ①).

River water stayed clean, even though people did not have toilets as we do now. Instead, when they wanted to go to the toilet they just wandered off into the forest.

The water remained safe because nature is very good at cleaning up waste like this, *provided there is not too much of it*. The soil is a natural filter, keeping any solid material from getting to the

► ① **Provided there were not too many people in an area, going to the toilet outside did not make the river water unclean because the soil contains natural purifiers.**

river. The soil and rocks also allow natural microbes to get to work and eat up the unhealthy germs in the waste.

The problem of many people

From the earliest times, people have known by experience that the safest water came from springs (picture ②). Many villages grew up at springs, and health towns – called **SPAS** – were founded because spring water was thought of as healthy.

Ever since the first cities were built, more water has been needed than a spring can provide. The answer was first solved in the land now called Pakistan. Here *deep* wells were sunk to get to the clean water buried in the rocks.

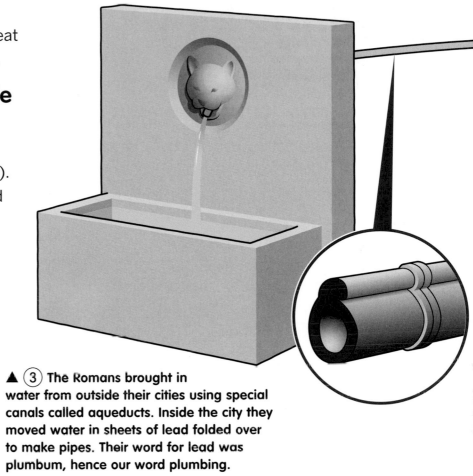

▲ ③ The Romans brought in water from outside their cities using special canals called aqueducts. Inside the city they moved water in sheets of lead folded over to make pipes. Their word for lead was plumbum, hence our word plumbing.

◄ ② Many small villages were founded near springs. The spring water was reliable – and more importantly, it was clean water.

In Roman times aqueducts were also used to bring clean water from the countryside to the cities. Inside the cities the water was carried to public fountains in pipes (picture ③). People then collected their water from these fountains.

By Roman times most people carried water from a fountain or from a common *deep* well. As a result it was clean and they did not have great problems with water-borne diseases.

Getting clean water: the years of disease

As more people crowded together, the need to keep sewage and drinking water apart became more vital. When this didn't happen, diseases spread.

After the Romans left things got worse, not better.

More people crowded into cities and more wells were dug. Many of these wells were *shallow*, because shallow wells are easier to dig than deep wells. At the same time, more and more sewage was simply tipped onto waste ground or into the streets (picture ②).

Little was done to take it away safely (picture ①) and so it seeped into the wells. As a result, more and more people began to be ill.

▲ ① By the 18th century the wealthy had water closets (but not flush toilets). The water carried the toilet waste out to a nearby pit, called a cesspit, where it was collected by 'soil men' at night. They simply tilled it into bigger cesspits which then overflowed to the rivers.

◄ ② In the Middle Ages, people did not have proper arrangements to deal with their toilet waste. Often they just tipped it into the streets. It then ran down gutters in the middle of the streets and found its way into rivers and into the ground. When people drank water from rivers or shallow wells they became ill.

Germs are found in water supplies

It was doctor John Snow, in London, who first proved a link between disease and water in 1854. He traced the outbreak of a disease called cholera and found that it was all connected to a single *shallow* well near the River Thames. When he stopped people from using the well, the disease went away.

Because the well was shallow, some sewage had seeped into it from pits nearby. People were drinking water filled with germs (picture ④).

Once the link was understood, the government began to organise proper toilets connected to sewers (picture ③). But early sewers still emptied directly into the rivers. It was only in 1858 – called "the Year of the Great Stink" – when the stench in the River Thames became so great that the politicians could not even stand to be in the Parliament building – that something was done.

Water is cleaned and separated from sewage

During the second part of the 19th century, water in cities was at last **PURIFIED** and then piped to people. Most importantly, it was kept entirely separate from sewage. This was done by making all sewage water flow through pipes to a sewage treatment works where the germs were killed. This is the system we still use today.

▼ ③ Victorian sewers were lined with brick. They were connected in a vast underground network.

◄ ④ Water often contains unseen germs, like these bacteria which cause the disease cholera.

Making water fit to drink

Water has to be made to look, taste and smell clean and have the germs removed.

If your water was brown, smelled of rotten eggs and had bits floating in it, would you drink it? The chances are you would think it was horrible.

Suppose we took the bits away, would you still drink it if it were only brown and smelled?

Now how about if we take the brown colour away. The water is crystal clear but still smells and tastes bad – are you satisfied yet?

We ask water companies to give us water which looks clear and has no smell or taste. But while we worry about things we can see and smell, we should also worry about what we can't see, for water can contain harmful chemicals that have no smell or colour, and germs so small that they cannot be seen. When water is clean it is called pure; anything stopping water from being pure is called an impurity.

How water is treated

Because water contains impurities, it has to be cleaned before we can drink it – even if it comes from a clean-looking river. This is what a drinking **WATER TREATMENT WORKS** is for (pictures ① and ②).

▲ ① **This is a water treatment works close to a reservoir.**

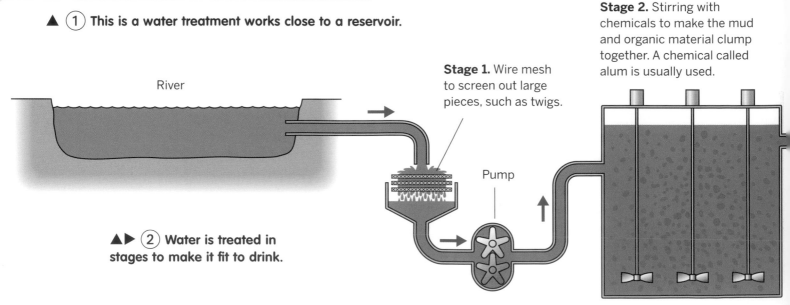

Stage 2. Stirring with chemicals to make the mud and organic material clump together. A chemical called alum is usually used.

Stage 1. Wire mesh to screen out large pieces, such as twigs.

River

Pump

▲▶ ② **Water is treated in stages to make it fit to drink.**

► ③ **This is the top of a settling tank (stage 3 in the diagram). Clean water flows into the trough, but it still contains enough dissolved material to let green algae grow. This must be removed by filters (stage 4 in the diagram).**

Water is pumped from the river and passed through a grating to trap the largest pieces, such as twigs and plastic bags (picture ② **Stage 1**).

The water still contains some grit, mud and **ORGANIC MATTER** (dead pieces of plants, algae, tiny water-living animals and so on). To get rid of most of these impurities, chemicals are added to the water and stirred (**Stage 2**). This is then transferred to a settling tank where mud and organic matter sink to the bottom (**Stage 3** and picture ③). This unwanted material makes a **SLUDGE**.

The water is now nearly pure. It is poured through a thick bed of sand and special charcoal granules to filter out any remaining particles, chemicals and colour (**Stage 4**). Helpful microbes in the sand also eat germs.

Finally, any harmful germs left in the water are killed. This is usually done by adding a chemical disinfectant called chlorine to the water (**Stage 5**).

Making the water clear, odour and taste-free

Removing germs

Stage 3. Allowing the clumped material to settle out.

Stage 4. Filtering out anything that remains using sand and charcoal.

Stage 5. Chlorine is added to the water to kill off any remaining germs.

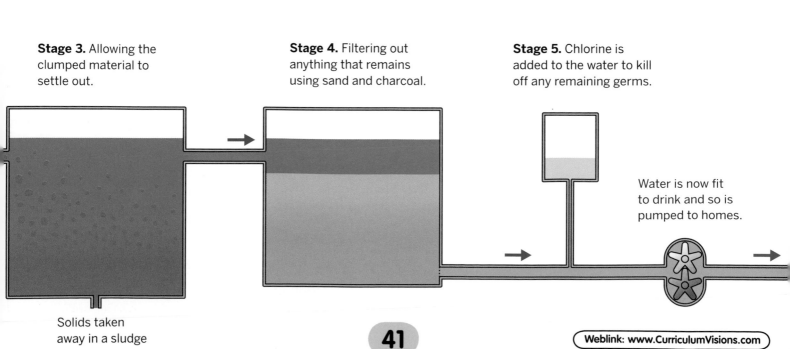

Water is now fit to drink and so is pumped to homes.

Solids taken away in a sludge

Weblink: www.CurriculumVisions.com

Cleaning the water we have used

Once we have made water dirty, we cannot forget about it. Instead, we have to collect it and clean it up. If we do not, the environment will suffer.

▲ ① **An engineer inspects a sample of polluted water before treatment in a sewage works.**

Sewage is water that is flushed from our toilets and sinks and which contains solids, chemicals and germs.

Sewage is far more polluted than the water taken from rivers for drinking (picture ①). Sewage includes: disease-carrying microbes brought from toilets, chemicals such as detergents and bleaches from washing up and cleaning, paper, plastic, metal, dirt, soil, grease and oil.

Treating the sewage

There is an old rhyme that "the solution to pollution is in dilution", which means that if you put a small amount of sewage (pollution) into a large amount of water (**DILUTION**), then the natural microbes in the water will eat the sewage and clean up the water naturally (the solution!).

Before you can do this, however, all of the solids must be removed. Large objects such as plastic bags, must be trapped and removed (picture ② **Stage 1**). Grit and sand are made to settle out at the bottom of big tanks. This material is taken to fill in old quarries (**Stage 2**).

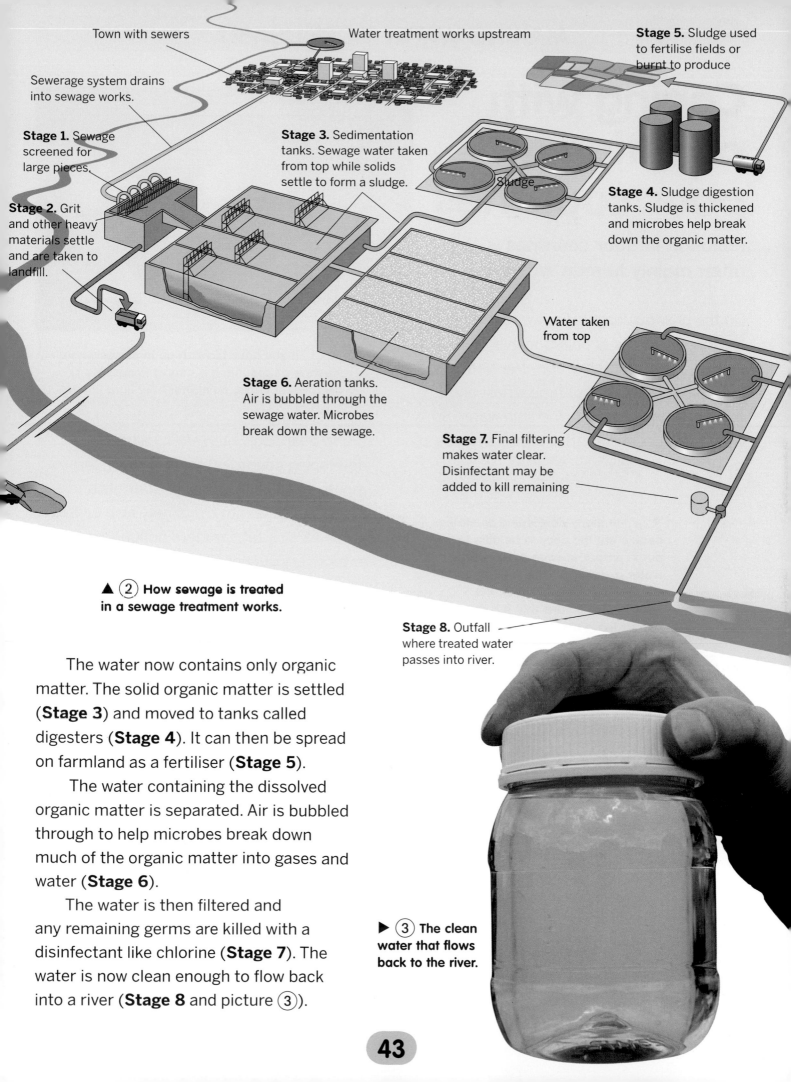

Town with sewers

Water treatment works upstream

Stage 5. Sludge used to fertilise fields or burnt to produce

Sewerage system drains into sewage works.

Stage 1. Sewage screened for large pieces.

Stage 3. Sedimentation tanks. Sewage water taken from top while solids settle to form a sludge.

Stage 2. Grit and other heavy materials settle and are taken to landfill.

Sludge

Stage 4. Sludge digestion tanks. Sludge is thickened and microbes help break down the organic matter.

Water taken from top

Stage 6. Aeration tanks. Air is bubbled through the sewage water. Microbes break down the sewage.

Stage 7. Final filtering makes water clear. Disinfectant may be added to kill remaining

▲ ② **How sewage is treated in a sewage treatment works.**

Stage 8. Outfall where treated water passes into river.

The water now contains only organic matter. The solid organic matter is settled (**Stage 3**) and moved to tanks called digesters (**Stage 4**). It can then be spread on farmland as a fertiliser (**Stage 5**).

The water containing the dissolved organic matter is separated. Air is bubbled through to help microbes break down much of the organic matter into gases and water (**Stage 6**).

The water is then filtered and any remaining germs are killed with a disinfectant like chlorine (**Stage 7**). The water is now clean enough to flow back into a river (**Stage 8** and picture ③).

▶ ③ **The clean water that flows back to the river.**

43

Coping with pollution in poor countries

Pollution in poor countries is often mainly human waste.

On the previous pages we saw that there are many sources of pollution even in a prosperous country like ours. We also saw that it takes a lot of time, effort and money to provide clean and safe water. So what happens in countries that are not as wealthy as ours?

▲ ① **If you have to wash up in places where waste is all around, it is almost impossible to keep water clean, no matter how hard you try.**

In poor countries (often called developing countries) there is much less money to clean up sewage. Controls on dumping waste into rivers may also be less strict. As a result, far more pollution can enter rivers or seep into the ground.

▼ ② **In many developing countries, people are too poor to be able to put in proper sewage pipes. Waste water is simply poured into an open channel that runs between the houses. This means that it is easy for people living nearby to get disease.**

Things can be done

Looking at the pictures on these pages, you might think that the task is impossible (pictures ①, ② and ③). But it is not. The easiest way to make water supplies cleaner is if sewage never gets into them. There are simple and cheap ways of doing this.

For example, deep pits can be dug in dry ground at least 250m from a water supply like a river. These are called pit **LATRINES** (picture ④). These are not as nice as the flush toilets we use, but they are still a big step forward, do an effective job and cost very little.

When one hole is filled up, the latrine hut can be moved to another hole. After a while, the waste in the used hole will have been broken down by nature and will be a clean, germ-free and valuable fertiliser. This is a cheap version of what a sewage works does.

▲ ③ For people living by a river or a lake, it is hard to get far enough away to deposit wastes safely. Often the wastes go into the same water that is used for washing up and drinking. In this picture, the toilet is in the foreground by the lake edge.

▶ ④ Pit latrines in use and pits dug for the future. Notice they are on high, dry ground away from rivers and houses.

Glossary

AQUEDUCT A canal, tunnel or pipe designed to carry water for drinking purposes.

Aqueducts have been in use since ancient times. Some of the largest modern aqueducts are in California, USA, where there is a great need to supply irrigation water to farmers and drinking water for cities such as Los Angeles. The California Aqueduct, for example, is over 700km long.

AQUIFER A water-bearing rock. Typical water-bearing rocks are chalk, limestone and sandstone. If the greater part of an aquifer is trapped between two layers of watertight rocks (aquicludes), the trapped water is called artesian water.

Aquifers are vital sources of drinking water in most countries of the world. However, they can be overused if the amount taken out is greater than the amount added by rainfall. When aquifers are overused, then the water is 'mined', and they will have a limited useful life before they dry up.

ARTESIAN WATER Groundwater that comes from an aquifer trapped between two watertight layers of rock. Water may seep into the aquifer where the rock is exposed in hills; but because it is confined between watertight layers, it has no means of escape. As a result, the water in an artesian aquifer is often under considerable pressure.

The world's largest artesian basin lies under much of northern central Australia.

CONDENSATION Water vapour condenses into liquid water when the temperature of the air falls. Air can cool because it comes into contact with a cold surface. This is why, for example, a glass containing ice cubes soon gathers a coating of condensation.

Air can also cool if it rises in the atmosphere. This is the reason clouds form.

DAM An artificial wall or embankment designed to hold back water. The water held back makes a reservoir (sometimes called a 'lake' if it is large).

Earth and rock dams are broad structures with gently sloping sides and a very wide base. Earth and rock are used only for dams of modest height. An earth dam is usually faced with stone so that it is not eroded by running water or lake waves. Masonry and concrete are used to build the world's tallest dams, or where a dam must be strong enough to block a narrow valley. The world's biggest dam is the Three Gorges dam on the Yangtze River in China.

DEVELOPING COUNTRY A country that does not have the wealth to provide many of the services, such as clean water, we take for granted.

DILUTE To reduce the concentration of a liquid by adding water.

DISINFECTANT A chemical that kills germs but is otherwise not harmful to people. Disinfectants are added to water supplies, usually in the form of chlorine.

DISTILLATION A process of heating water so that the water evaporates, leaving any pollution behind. The water vapour is then cooled, so that it condenses and turns back into pure liquid water.

DRINKING WATER Water that is safe to drink. Very strict regulations are in place in many countries to make sure that drinking water is of the highest quality and does not contain poisonous substances, pieces of soil, or disease-carrying organisms.

Drinking water has to be both clarified (made to look clean) and purified (disinfected) by the time it reaches taps. This is a complicated and expensive process.

DROUGHT An unusually long period without significant rainfall.

Some parts of the world, particularly between latitudes 10° and 35°, have a more variable rainfall pattern than others, and so they can be said to be more drought-prone. These places include the Sahel region of Africa just south of the Sahara Desert, southern Africa, northeast Brazil, Australia, the southwestern United States and India. Some places have seasons when rain never falls. They are called dry seasons, but they are not droughts. In these areas droughts occur in the rainy season when the rains do not fall as normal.

EVAPORATION The change of water from liquid to vapour at temperatures below boiling.

FLOOD Floods occur whenever water flows across normally dry land. Both rivers and seas can cause flooding.

To either side of a river channel there is flat land which has been made by the river during previous floods. This is called a floodplain. Anything built on the floodplain – no matter how far it might be from the river – will be flooded from time to time.

Floods are not just water. All floodwaters carry huge amounts of sediment with them.

GERMS Tiny living things – known as microbes – that can cause illness. Many germs are taken into the body through the water supply. Germs can be killed with disinfectants or by boiling. Because most natural waters contain germs, they are, in general, not safe to drink without first being treated.

GROUNDWATER The water held within water-bearing rocks, or aquifers, in the ground.

Water may flow naturally to the surface and come out as a spring, bubble upward as a flowing pool, or it may be taken out of the rocks by using a well or a bore hole.

Limestone, chalk, and sandstone are the main rocks that are permeable enough for groundwater to flow through them readily. Water that is trapped in aquifers is called artesian water. It is a particularly important source of water in dry areas, but is exploited in all parts of the world.

HYDROELECTRIC POWER STATION

A power station that produces electricity by forcing water to turn turbine blades which are connected to a shaft which turns an electric generator.

IRRIGATION The supply of water to farmland so that crops can grow in areas where natural water supplies are scarce or unreliable.

Water for irrigation comes either from groundwater supplies or from reservoirs and river diversions. See also aqueduct.

In dry countries irrigation can use more water than all other demands (home, industry, power) put together.

LATRINE A pit in the ground intended to be used as a toilet.

OASIS (*pl* **OASES**) A reliable natural spring in a desert.

Oases are fed by springs flowing from rocks. The source of the spring may be hundreds of kilometres away from the spring in a place where water is more plentiful, such as a mountain range.

Many oases are very small, but some can be hundreds of square kilometers in area.

ORGANIC MATTER Food and toilet wastes.

POLLUTED WATER Water that is unfit for its intended purpose.

PURIFY (PURIFICATION) To clean water so that it becomes fit for its intended purpose.

RESERVOIR An artificial lake created by building a dam across a river. Some reservoirs are called lakes because of their size.

River flows naturally vary through the year, so that there may be more water than can be used at one time of year and too little at another. During periods of heavy rainfall rivers may also swell and burst their banks, leading to widespread destruction. Reservoirs are built to control the flow of water in a river to prevent flooding and to give a reliable flow of water through the year.

Reservoirs are used for providing drinking water, for irrigation water and for hydroelectric power.

SEWAGE TREATMENT WORKS

A place designed to treat wastes in public water supplies. It consists of stages of getting rid of contaminants and stages of disinfecting.

SEWER A large pipe designed to handle water-borne wastes from toilets, baths, sinks, and so on.

SLUDGE The solid material, mostly organic matter, that settles out of water while it is being purified.

SPA A town developed around the supposed health-giving waters of a spring. Bath and Buxton are spa towns.

SPRING A place where water naturally seeps or gushes from the ground.

Springs are fed by groundwater. They occur in aquifers, often where a river cuts down to the water table. Other springs happen where a permeable rock is over a layer of impermeable rock. This sometimes gives rise to 'weeping cliffs', as water seeps from the base of the permeable rock.

Bubbling or swiftly flowing springs are not especially common. Most rivers begin with muddy patches on a hillside rather than a bubbling spring.

WATER COMPANY A company whose main job is to provide clean water and to deal with sewage.

WATER CYCLE The circulation of water between the seas, the air, the plants, the rocks and the rivers. The energy for this, the world's greatest cycle, comes from the Sun and gravity. The energy of the Sun allows evaporation and powers the winds that carry moist air from the oceans to the land, while gravity brings water back from the clouds and rivers to the oceans.

The water cycle is the main means of transferring water in the world.

WATER TREATMENT WORKS

A place designed to treat water from, for example, a river or a lake, and purify it so that it is suitable for drinking.

WELL A vertical shaft that is drilled down into an aquifer in order to obtain water for drinking and other home uses, for industry or for farming.

A small well meant to serve a single house may be about 1m across and be lined with brick. Water is drawn by a bucket or a small pump.

The wells needed to supply water to a city are on an altogether different scale. These wells are often sunk many hundreds of metres down into a large, reliable aquifer. They are not open wells, but enclosed, and with pipes about 30cm across. These wells are sealed so that the clean water coming from the well is not contaminated from the surface. The water is pumped out of the aquifer using high-power pumps.

Weblink: www.CurriculumVisions.com

Index

SOCK FRIENDS Craft Book

TOP THAT

Licensed exclusively to Top That Publishing Ltd
Tide Mill Way, Woodbridge, Suffolk, IP12 1AP, UK
www.topthatpublishing.com
Copyright © 2015 Tide Mill Media
2 4 6 8 9 7 5 3 1
Manufactured in China

Sock Friends

Get ready to turn ordinary socks into a collection
of sock puppet friends for hours of creative play!

Before you start …

Before you start, check out
the list at the beginning
of each project and gather
together everything you need.
That means you'll be ready to
get making sock puppet friends
straight away!

Using templates

Some of the projects are made
using templates. Use tracing
paper and a pencil to transfer
them onto white paper. Cut them
out and pin them onto felt, then
cut around the edges.

Items you'll need

The most important things you'll
need are socks! You could use old
socks of your own, or buy new
ones especially for the job.

You can buy everything else you
need, such as felt, pompoms and
fuzzy sticks, from craft and
hobby shops, or online. You'll
probably find some useful items
around the home, too.

For every project, make sure
you have a pair of scissors,
some glue and felt-tip pens or
pencils handy.

Imaginative ideas

The step-by-step instructions
should be used only as a guide
to making the puppets, so don't
worry about following them
exactly. It's fun to experiment
with ideas and materials of
your own!

Top Tips

Follow these top tips for amazing sock puppet friends every time!

• Sometimes you'll need to decorate your puppet whilst it's on your hand, especially when you're creating the mouth. To keep both hands free at other times, stretch your sock puppet over a cardboard tube, or borrow someone else's hand!

• Use felt or material scraps, coloured paper, card or tissue paper to decorate your sock puppets. Wool and thread make good hair, and bracelets can be used as necklaces.

• Keep any offcuts of felt. These come in handy for cutting out eyes, teeth and horns.

• Look for beads, sequins, buttons and scraps of ribbon to decorate your sock puppets.

• A pot of elastic bands and safety pins are good for pinching and gathering in material.

Warning:
Scissors and fuzzy sticks have sharp points. Use under direct adult supervision.

Baa! Baa!

Clipper the Sheep

1 Place the sock over your hand. Put your fingers in the toe piece and your thumb in the heel. Take a large piece of cotton wool, place it inside the sock and pad out the toe piece until it is full.

3 Cut two long ear shapes out of the black felt. Tuck these under the elastic band on both sides.

Tip: Draw an ear onto a piece of paper first and when you are happy with the shape, cut it out and use it as a template for the felt.

2 Tie an elastic band around the nose, just in front of your fingers. This will make a rounded nose. Mould the cotton wool until you have the desired shape, as shown.

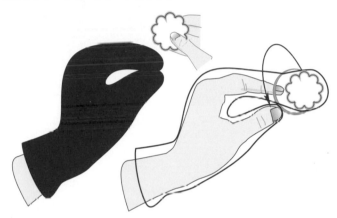

4 Next, cut two small black circles from the black felt. Glue the two large white pompoms onto the face, covering the elastic band, and leave to dry. Take the two black felt circles and glue one to the front of each pompom for the sheep's pupils.

Tip: You could make card eyes like the ones opposite instead.

5

5 Next, take the two small black pompoms and glue them onto the end of the nose for the sheep's nostrils.

6 To make the sheep's woolly coat, glue three cotton wool balls to the top of the head, directly behind the eyes.

7 Then, turn the puppet round and glue three more balls behind the first row, at the back of the head. Leave to dry.

Tip: Try to use glue in a tube for this, rather than glue on a brush. This way you can just squeeze out a blob of glue at a time without touching the cotton wool.

8 Cut out a black felt semicircle that fits the head, as shown. Glue it to the front of the cotton wool, behind the eyes. This will create the sheep's head.

9 Take more cotton wool balls and, starting at the front, under the nose, glue rows all the way round your sheep. When the entire body is covered, leave to dry thoroughly.

Tip: Leave a gap between the head and the body. This will allow you to manoeuvre your puppet easily.

10 Draw a leg shape onto a piece of paper and when you are happy with it, cut it out and use it as a template for the felt. Cut out two legs.

11 Carefully part the cotton wool balls on the left side of the sheep's body. Glue the leg onto the sock, sandwiching it between the cotton balls. Repeat this for the right leg, and leave to dry.

12 To finish, ask an adult to spray all of the cotton wool with hairspray. This will help to stop it coming apart. Make sure you do this in a well ventilated area.

ADULT HELP REQUIRED!

Where does a sheep go for a haircut? The Baabaas!

I'm such a friendly monster!

Nessie of Loch Ness

Tip: Choose pompoms to complement your choice of sock. We have used purple and green to match our colours, but you can choose whatever colours you like!

1 Place the sock over your hand. Put your fingers in the toe piece, with the heel on top of your hand. Take a large piece of cotton wool, and place it inside the toe of the sock. This will make a nice rounded nose.

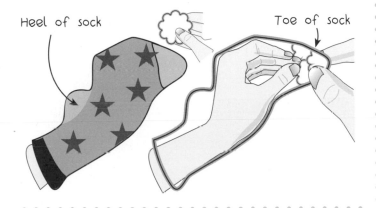

Heel of sock

Toe of sock

2 Take a smaller piece of cotton wool. Place it in the centre, inside the sock, and against the back of your fingers. Pinch the cotton wool and tie an elastic band round it to create the first hump.

3 Next, take more cotton wool and fill out the heel of the sock. Shape it to create your monster's second hump! For the third hump, repeat step 2 at the base of the sock, as shown below.

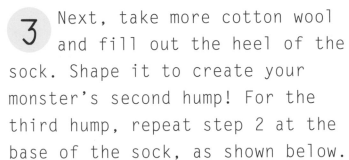

4 Glue two large pompoms to the front of the first hump. Then, glue two small pompoms in front of them. Cut out two small semicircles of white felt.

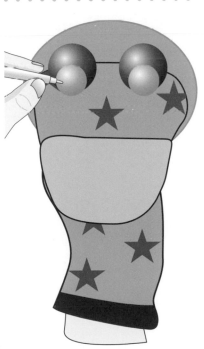

Tip: If you don't have any felt, use a piece of white card!

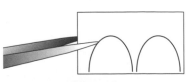

5 Glue the two white pieces of felt to the front of the small pompoms and, using a black felt-tip pen, colour in the pupils.

6 Next, glue two more small pompoms onto the nose for the nostrils. Add a tiny pompom on the end of each of these.

7 To make the horn, glue three tiny pompoms onto two small pompoms. When dry, glue this to the middle of the head.

8 Take the fuzzy stick and cut it in half. Bend one half of the fuzzy stick around the eyes to make eyebrows and glue in place.

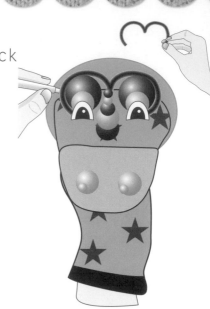

Warning: Ask an adult to cut and bend the fuzzy stick as these can be quite sharp!

9 Take the two coloured felt pieces. Cut out a semicircle from one colour then, using the other colour, cut out a tongue. Glue the tongue onto the semicircle. Open your sock and glue the felt piece in the centre for the mouth.

10 Take the remaining three large pompoms, glue one to the top of each hump and leave to dry.

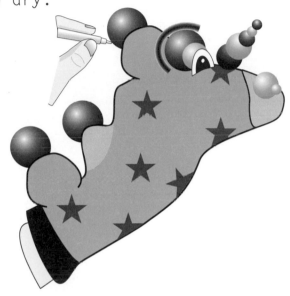

11 Take the six remaining small pompoms and glue one on each side of the large pompoms on each hump, as shown. Leave to dry.

12 When all of the pompoms are dry, take the remaining piece of fuzzy stick and bend it around the third hump. Glue in place. This will cover the elastic band.

What did the Loch Ness Monster say to his friend? Long time no sea!

You will need

- An old cereal box
- Pencil
- Paper
- Scissors
- A blue sock
- Cotton wool
- Glue
- Tracing paper
- One piece of red felt
- One piece of white felt
- Two black buttons
- Black felt-tip pen
- One piece of blue felt

Chomp!
Chomp!

Razor the Shark

1 First, flatten out the cereal box. Place your wrist and hand on top of it, then trace around both. Cut the shape out of the card, rounding off the fingers and thumb, as shown. Put your hand in the sock, fingers in the toe and thumb in the heel. Put the card inside the sock, on top of your hand, to create the basic shark shape.

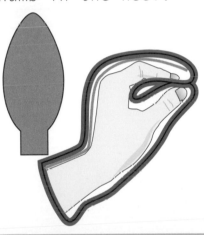

Tip: If you are using a large sock for any project in this book, you will need an adult's hand to trace around.

2 Take a large piece of cotton wool. Place it in the toe, inside the sock, and on top of the card shape. Add cotton wool until you have filled the sock down to the back of your hand, shaping it as you go.

3 To create the pointed snout, pull the sides of the sock in tight underneath your fingers. Glue in place and then leave to dry.

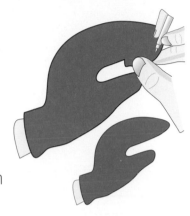

Tip: If you can't wait for the glue to dry, ask an adult to secure the snout by sewing it together with a couple of stitches.

4 To make the shark's mouth and tongue, trace the templates on page 32, cut them out and place them on the red felt. Draw around them, then cut out the felt shapes. Open up your sock and glue the red oval inside to make the mouth, as shown above.

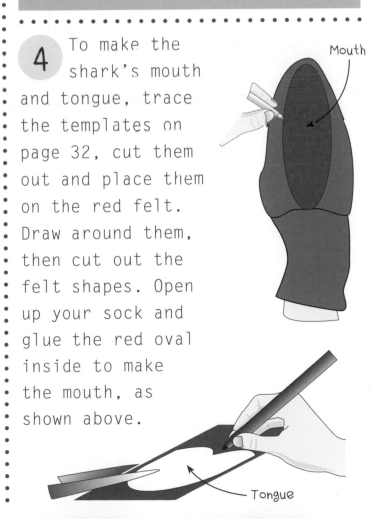

Mouth

Tongue

5 To make the teeth, trace the templates on page 32 and cut them out. Place them on the white felt, draw around them and cut out the shapes. Glue the teeth around the mouth, as shown, then glue the tongue in place.

Teeth

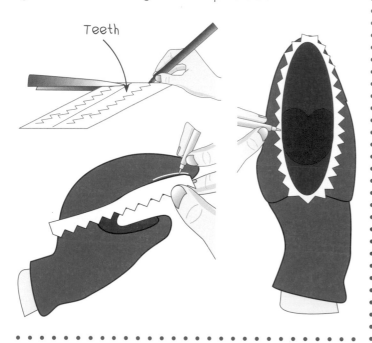

7 Trace the big fin, small fins and gills from page 32 and cut them out. Place them on the blue felt, draw around them and cut out the shapes.

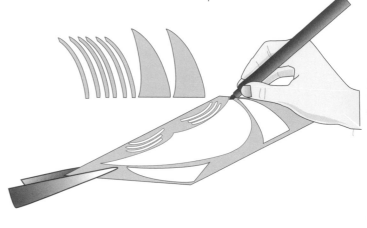

8 Take the big fin and place some cotton wool in the centre. Glue around the edge and fold it over, sandwiching the cotton wool in the middle. Glue this onto the shark's back. Leave to dry.

6 Glue a black button on each side of the head for the eyes. Using a felt-tip pen, draw the nostril holes on either side of the snout.

Tip: You could add tiny white felt circles for highlights to the eyes.

9 To make the tummy, trace the template from page 32, cut it out and draw around it on the white felt. Cut out the felt shape and glue it under the mouth.

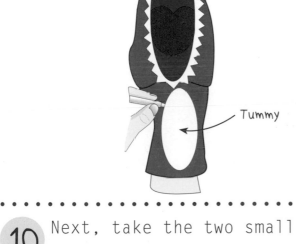

Tummy

10 Next, take the two small fins cut out earlier and glue one on each side of the white oval.

11 To finish your shark, glue on the six gills cut out earlier, three on either side of the face.

Now that's a project you can really sink your teeth into!

Snap! Snap!

You will need

- A red sock
- Cotton wool
- Glue
- Two small red pompoms
- Two elastic bands
- Red fuzzy stick
- Two large yellow pompoms
- Two large red pompoms
- One piece of white felt
- Black felt-tip pen
- Red card
- Yellow felt
- Paper
- Glitter

Snap the Dragon

1 Place the sock over your hand. Put your fingers in the toe piece and your thumb in the heel. Take a small piece of cotton wool and glue it inside the toe of the sock, in the centre. Poke your finger into the cotton wool and shape it into a pointy end.

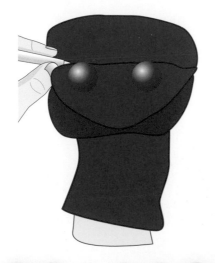

2 Using the two small red pompoms, glue them on either side of the nose to create the dragon's nostrils.

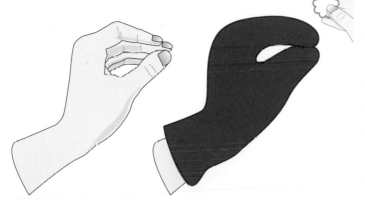

3 Pinch a piece of sock on the side of the head, twist it and tie an elastic band around it. Repeat this on the other side of the head for the ears.

4 Take the red fuzzy slick and ask an adult to cut it in half. Twist one half around one of the ears, covering the elastic band. Repeat this for the other ear.

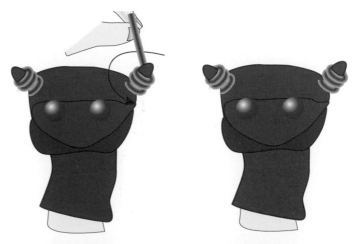

5 Glue the large yellow pompoms onto the face in between the ears. Then, glue the two large red pompoms in front of them.

6 Cut out two small semicircles of white felt. Glue these in front of the red pompoms and use a black felt-tip pen to colour in the pupils.

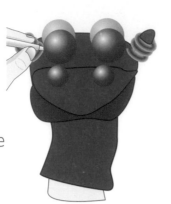

7 To make the horns and teeth, cut four triangle shapes from the white felt. Glue the horns on top of the yellow pompoms. Glue the teeth on either side of the mouth.

8 Take the red card and draw a wing shape onto it. Cut this out, trace around it onto more red card and cut out the second wing.

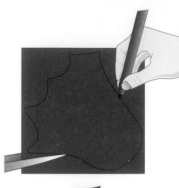

9 Take the yellow felt and draw on some flames. The flames should be about the same width as the mouth and slightly longer. Then cut them out. Place the wings and flames onto a sheet of paper, draw lines of glue along the wings and flames and sprinkle these with glitter. Leave to dry.

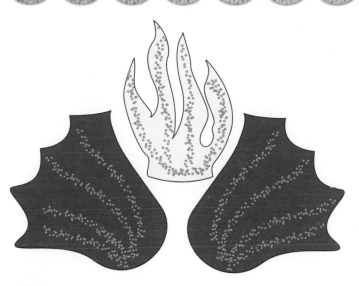

11 To finish, glue a wing onto each side of the dragon.

10 Take the flames and glue them into the centre of the mouth. The flames should stick out between the teeth when your hand is closed. Leave to dry.

Knock, knock! Who's there? Dragon! Dragon who? Dragon your feet again!

Zog the Alien

1 Place the sock over your hand. Your fingers should be in the toe piece and your thumb in the heel. Bend your thumb to create a basic mouth shape.

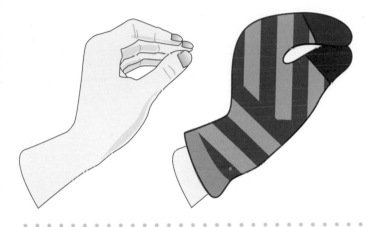

2 Take a small piece of cotton wool. Place it inside the sock, against the back of your fingers where they bend, until you have a little lump. Pinch the lump and tie the elastic band around it to create the main eye.

3 Glue the large goggly eye to the centre of the lump made on the head to complete your alien's main eye.

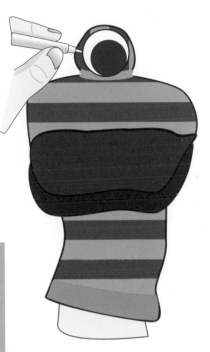

Tip: You could make your own goggly eyes using white card circles and a black felt-tip pen.

4 Take a silver fuzzy stick and ask an adult to cut it into three equal pieces. Bend one of the pieces into a zigzag shape (an antenna), tuck it under the elastic band and bend over the end to secure it. Repeat for the other antenna.

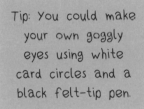

5 Next, glue the large red pompoms onto the antennae, as shown.

6 Take the remaining piece of fuzzy stick and bend it into an arch. Glue this on either side of the main eye, glue two small red pompoms on each side and then four more across the nose.

7 Take the two small goggly eyes and glue them onto the two small red pompoms.

8 To make the mouth, trace the template from page 32 and cut it out. Place it on the red felt, draw around it and cut the shape out.

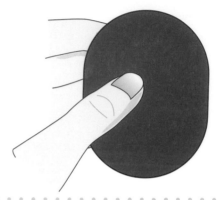

9 To make the teeth, trace the templates from page 32, cut them out and transfer them to white felt. Place the felt shapes in pairs, as shown. Place a piece of cotton wool between each pair, then glue around the edges, sandwiching the cotton wool in the middle. Leave to dry.

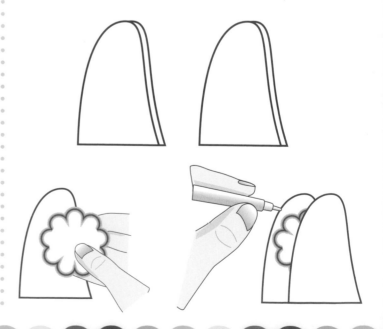

22

10 When the teeth are dry, open up your sock and glue the red felt piece in the centre for the mouth and the two teeth on either side. When you close your sock, the teeth should stick out on either side.

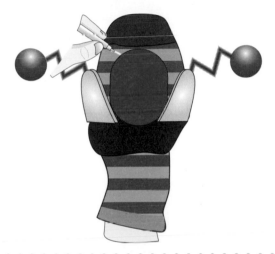

11 Take the remaining silver fuzzy stick and glue it underneath the mouth. Leave to dry.

12 When the fuzzy stick is dry, bend it into shape and glue on a green pompom where each arm leaves the body. To finish, glue two green pompoms on each end of the fuzzy stick to create the hands.

I'm Posie!

To make Posie you will need
- A large pink sock
- Cotton wool
- An elastic band
- Cereal box
- Black felt-tip pen
- Scissors
- Scrap of pink felt
- Glue
- Two pink buttons
- Scraps of white, blue & dark pink felt
- A black fuzzy stick
- A black feather
- 5 cm square of pale pink felt
- 4 cm squares of dark pink felt
- Yellow thread
- Pink fuzzy stick
- White tissue paper or a frill top sock

I'm Petal!

To make Petal you will need
- Pink baby's lace top sock
- Cotton wool • An elastic band
- An old cereal box • Felt-tip pen
- Scissors • Scrap of dark pink felt
- Glue • Pink button • Two goggly eyes
- 4 cm square of pale pink felt
- 3 cm square of dark pink felt
- Half a pink fuzzy stick

Posie and Petal Pig

Posie Pig

1 Place the sock over your hand. Put your fingers in the toe piece (the heel should be on the top of your hand). Take a large piece of cotton wool and place it inside the toe of the sock. Pinch the lump and form it into a ball. Then, tie the elastic band around it to create Posie's snout.

Heel of sock

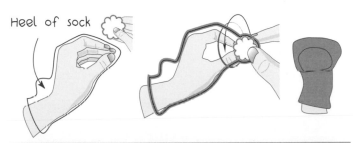

Tip: Don't tie the elastic band too tight. You will need enough room to get your fingers in to manoeuvre your puppet.

2 Take more of the cotton wool and fill out the sock behind the snout, shaping it into a head. Then draw a circle, roughly the same size, onto a cereal box. Cut it out, then ask an adult

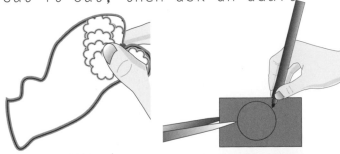

to cut a small piece out of the bottom of the circle so you can get your middle finger through to the snout. Place it inside the sock.

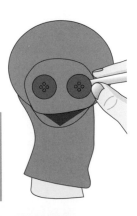

3 Poke your middle finger in the snout and keep your hand behind the card. Stick your thumb into the sock to create the basic mouth shape. Take a scrap of pink felt and cut out a triangle. Glue this under the snout to make the inside of the mouth (see step 4).

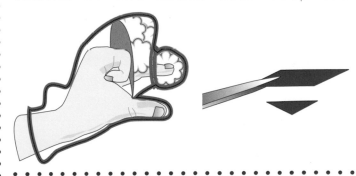

4 Glue two pink buttons onto the snout and leave to dry.

Tip: If you don't have any pink buttons, try using two pompoms, or two circles of felt or coloured card.

5 For the eyes you will need to cut two of each of the following: a large and small circle of white felt, a medium blue circle of felt, a semicircle of dark pink felt, a piece of black fuzzy stick and a black feather. Assemble the eyes, as shown above, gluing each piece as you go. Leave to dry.

Tip: Don't forget to place the fuzzy stick the other way for the left eye.

6 When the eyes are completely dry, glue them onto the face above the snout.

7 For the ears, cut the 5 cm and 4 cm pink felt squares in half so you have two large pale pink triangles and two smaller dark pink triangles.

Place the dark pink triangle on top of the pale pink one, and fold in both corners to the centre. Then, fold in half. Glue along the bottom edge and leave to dry. Repeat for the second ear.

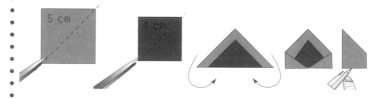

8 When the ears are dry, open them out and glue one on either side of the head, as shown.

9 Take the yellow thread and fold it over until you have the desired length of hair. Glue it to your sock puppet's head, then trim the ends.

10 Take a piece of the cotton wool and fill out the heel of the sock. Shape it to create your pig's bottom!

11 Wind the pink fuzzy stick around a pen, then slide it off gently. Glue the curly tail to the top of the pig's bottom.

12 Wrap a strip of tissue paper twice around your pig whilst it is on your hand to ensure you have enough. Now carefully pleat the piece of tissue and glue it around your pig, gathering it as you go to make a frilly tutu.

Alternatively, you can cut the top off a frilly sock and use that instead. We added a beaded bracelet as a necklace.

Petal Pig

Use a baby's sock, then repeat the steps that you followed to make Posie. Use just one button for the snout and leave out the 'eyes' step. (Just stick on two goggly eyes.) You don't have to add the hair and you can use the frill on the sock as the tutu. Easy peasy!

These little piggies went to the ballet!

27

You will need
- A green sock
- Cotton wool
- Three elastic bands
- Two large white pompoms
- Two small black pompoms
- Glue
- Black fuzzy stick
- Two small green pompoms
- Scissors
- One piece of black felt
- One piece of red felt
- Darning needle
- One ball of green wool
- An empty tube
- Tinfoil
- Ruler
- Cocktail stick
- Card

Hello everyone!

28

Trashy the Monster

1 Place the sock over your hand. Your fingers should be in the toe piece and your thumb in the heel. Bend your thumb to create a basic mouth shape.

2 Take a large piece of cotton wool and place it inside the toe of the sock. Add cotton wool until you have filled the toe piece, shaping it into a sausage. Tie an elastic band around it to create the top lip.

3 Take a small piece of cotton wool. Place it behind the top lip, slightly to the left, until you have a little lump. Pinch the lump and tie an elastic band around it to create the left eye. Repeat for the right eye.

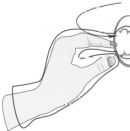

4 Next, add cotton wool behind the eye sockets to create a round head.

5 Glue two large white pompoms onto the two eye bulges. Then, glue small black pompoms onto the white pompoms for the pupils. Bend the black fuzzy stick around the eye sockets for eyebrows and glue in place.

Warning: Ask an adult to bend the ends of the fuzzy stick as these can be quite sharp!

6 To make the lower lip, fill the heel of the sock with cotton wool and shape this into a sausage.

7 The inside of the mouth will have an excess of sock material. Carefully pull the excess over the top lip and glue along the edge to keep it in place. (This will give you a pocket to put your fingers in.)

8 Glue the two small green pompoms onto the top lip to create nostrils.

9 Cut an oval shape out of black felt, open up your hand and glue it on the inside of the mouth. Then, cut a tongue shape from the red felt and glue it onto the black oval.

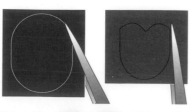

10 For the hair, first thread the darning needle with a length of green wool. Starting at the top and back of the puppet's head, push the needle into the sock and pull it through, leaving a small tail of wool sticking out. Loop the wool around your index finger, then push the needle into the sock, just behind the previous stitch, and pull it through. Repeat this until you have completed a row, working back down the head. Carefully remove your finger from the stitches and cut down the centre loops with scissors. Tie each thread in a knot to secure it, as shown.

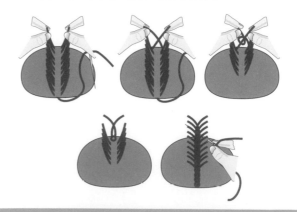

Tip: You may need an adult to help you with this, as it can be a bit fiddly!

11 When you have completed a row, start a new row alongside it. Repeat until you have covered the entire head.

12 To make the trash can, take an empty tube and cover it in glue. Cover the tube with tinfoil and tuck over the edges, making sure they are well stuck down.

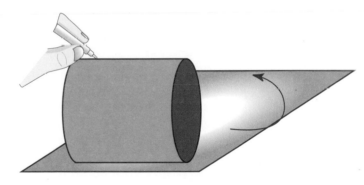

Note: Your hand must be able to fit inside the tube!

13 With a ruler, measure and draw lines around the tube. Use a cocktail stick to inscribe the lines.

14 For the lid, cut a circle from some card, scrunch up tinfoil and glue it to the circle, then cover the whole lid in tinfoil.

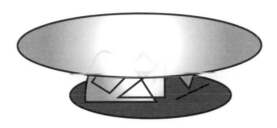

Roll up another piece of tinfoil, bend it into an arch and glue it on top. Finally, glue this onto your monster's head.

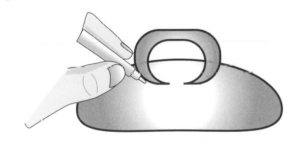

Yum, yum, rubbish for my tum!

Templates

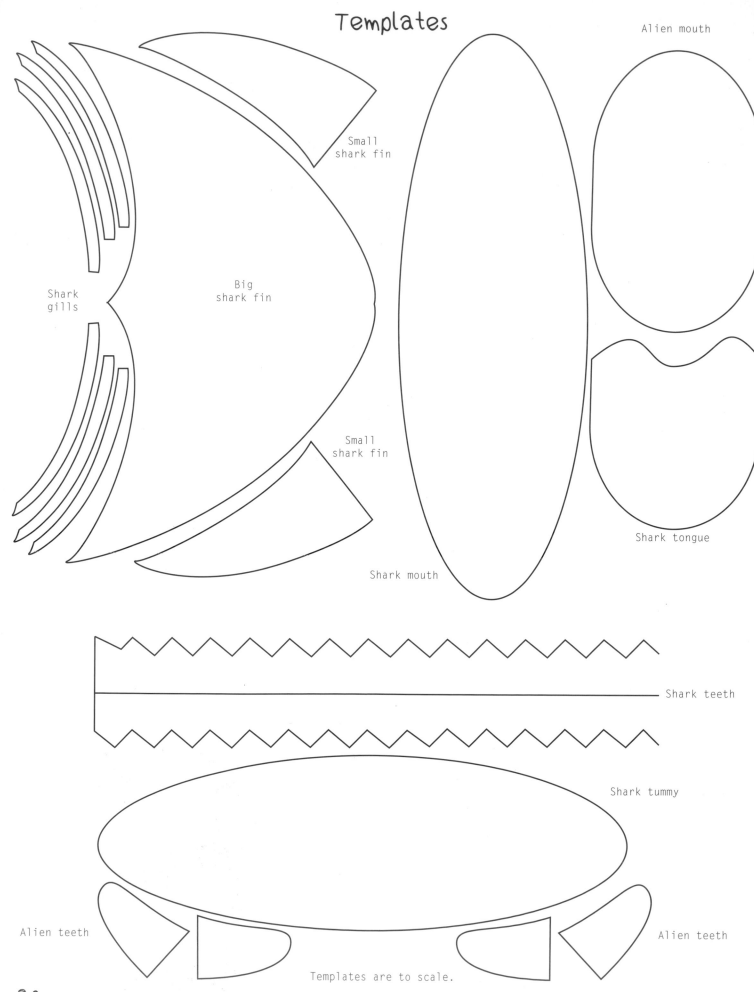

Alien mouth

Small
shark fin

Shark
gills

Big
shark fin

Small
shark fin

Shark tongue

Shark mouth

Shark teeth

Shark tummy

Alien teeth

Alien teeth

Templates are to scale.

32